Sports Illustrated
SKIING

The Sports Illustrated Library

BOOKS ON TEAM SPORTS

Baseball	Basketball	Ice Hockey	Football

BOOKS ON INDIVIDUAL SPORTS

Badminton	Horseback Riding	Skiing
Fencing	The Shotgun	Squash
Gaited Riding	Shotgun Sports	Tennis
Golf	Track and Field: Running Events	Wet-Fly Fishing

BOOKS ON WATER SPORTS

Better Boating	Junior Sailing	Swimming
Diving	Small Boat Sailing	

SPECIAL BOOKS

Dog Training	Safe Driving

Sports Illustrated
SKIING

By JOHN JEROME
and the Editors of
Sports Illustrated

J. B. LIPPINCOTT COMPANY
Philadelphia and New York

ISBN-0-397-00840-6 Cloth Edition
ISBN-0-397-00839-2 Paper Edition

Copyright © 1971 by Time, Inc.
New edition
Printed in the United States of America
Library of Congress Catalog Card No.: 71–146685

Fourth Printing

Photographs from *Sports Illustrated,*
© Time, Inc.

Photographs by John G. Zimmerman:
Cover and page 58: "Out of Sight"
Page 12: "Tourist Trap, Vail"
Page 20: "Alta Powder"
Page 26: "Spring Corn, Mt. Hood"
Page 50: "The First Turns, Vail"
Page 72: "The Bugaboos, British Columbia"

Photograph by Marvin E. Newman:
Page 88: "Jean-Claude Killy"

Contents

Introduction　9

1. THE PHYSICAL REQUIREMENTS　13
   THE EXERCISES　14
   　　TOE TOUCHING　14
   　　ANKLE BENDS　15
   　　TORSO TWISTING　15
   　　TORSO BENDS　16
   　　EDGING　16
   　　SPLITS　17
   　　TOE PULLS　17
   　　BACK BENDS　18
   　　NECK ROLLS　18
   A PROGRAM　19

2. THE EQUIPMENT REVOLUTION　21

3. FOR BEGINNERS ONLY　27

4. THE BASICS　35
   BALANCE AND STANCE　36
   EDGE CONTROL　40
   SIDESLIPPING　42

TRAVERSING 45

THE SNOWPLOW 47

5. THE FIRST TURNS 51

SNOWPLOW TURN 51

CHRISTIE INTO THE HILL 53

STEM TURN 55

SQUARE VS. REVERSED SHOULDER 61

HOW A SKI TURNS 63

THE STEM CHRISTIE 65

STEM CHRISTIE WITH A DOWNHILL STEM 69

HOW CLOSE TOGETHER? 69

6. CHRISTIES 73

UNWEIGHTING 75

TURNING FORCE 80

EDGE RELEASE 80

THE SKI POLE 84

7. PUTTING IT ALL TOGETHER 89

HOW TO HANDLE SOME SPECIFIC PROBLEMS 91

MOGULS 91

ICE 91

SOFT SNOW 94

FLAT LIGHT 96

STEEP SLOPE 96

Illustrations by Frank Mullins

Sports Illustrated
SKIING

Introduction

WATCH an active seven-year-old take up the sport of skiing, and you will get an object lesson in how to go about learning to ski. The youngster won't stand still for complications; he is only interested in having fun and in being able to go anywhere he wants on skis. He *has* to grasp the fundamentals of the sport quickly—otherwise he might miss out on some of the fun.

Similarly, if you analyze a film of a ski racer plunging down a racing course, you will find that he may well violate all the sacred canons of formalized ski instruction on any one run. He still gets down the mountain in absolute control, at breakneck speed. The ski racer, like the seven-year-old, is simply and directly motivated. The learning process for both skiers doesn't allow for dogma. Results count for more than style.

The racer and the seven-year-old represent a kind of New Wave in skiing, which is best summed up by the simple term *naturalness*. Ski instruction in this country is almost forty years old, and most of those years have been spent in argument over whether to split hairs from the bottom up or from the top down. Now, emphasis has begun to shift away from this internecine warfare between ski teachers, and toward preparing the skier to have a good time on the slopes. The fundamentals—how to turn when and where you want to; how to control your speed, stop, and get down the hill without hurting yourself—are generally understood. These fundamentals remain basically the same whether you approach them through the American technique of ski teaching or that of the Austrians, the French or the Transylvanians. The goal is to stand naturally on your skis, adjust your weight and attitude to the conditions that arise and deal with the problems of speed, snow and terrain as you most comfortably can. When you can do that much easily, you can then begin to polish the details.

The American Ski Technique was devised by the Professional Ski Instructors of America, in order to bring a degree of rationality to ski teaching in this country. Because most of the ski schools in the United States have adopted the American Ski Technique, it is possible for skiers to attend classes at various ski schools, at different ski areas, without running into a confusion of techniques. France, Austria, Switzerland, Italy, Canada and Japan also have national ski techniques, consistent within national boundaries but at odds with their skiing neighbors. The differences, fortunately, are usually in details rather than in fundamentals.

There has been no attempt, therefore, to restrict the skiing methods explained in this book to the strict parameters of any single nationality. We have no interest in promulgating tunnel vision with regard to skiing skills. Our view is that the doctrinaire approach is out and fun is in. Skiing is, after all, a sport. The object is not to duplicate the exquisite picture the expert makes as he skis, but to learn to handle the mountain as well as he does. That concept guides this book.

Billy Kidd, who skis for Frank Mullins' illustrations in the following pages, is the first American man to win a medal in Olympic ski racing and the first to win a gold medal in world championship competition. He began skiing at five, won the silver medal for slalom at Innsbruck in the 1964 Winter Olympics and then suffered a six-year injury-ridden slump. In 1970, at twenty-six the "old man" of the U.S. Ski Team came back, placing third in the slalom, fifteenth in the giant slalom, and fifth in the downhill at the F.I.S. World Championships at Val Gardena, Italy. That performance was good enough for the overall win. Billy was awarded the gold medal for the Men's Combined, signifying him the best ski racer in the world in 1970. From Stowe, Vermont, Billy now lives in Boulder, Colorado.

1
The Physical Requirements

MODERN skiing is easy, loose, natural, rhythmic in style—characteristics seldom duplicated by the jangling tensions of much of the rest of modern life. The great popularity, in recent years, of physical fitness and conditioning programs is doing wonders in building strength and stamina and in re-depositing extra weight and girth in more seemly areas of the body. Unfortunately, such programs seldom deal with the problems of stiffness and tension. They don't do an adequate job of developing the suppleness and elasticity that skiing requires.

A preseason conditioning program is invaluable to the skier. Push-ups, sit-ups, knee bends, chinning, jogging, are all great; more power to them. But to get the most out of your skiing time—to help prevent lost skiing days as a result of sore muscles, and also to help you avoid injury from an occasional tumble—it is recommended that you add to a conventional conditioning program the following skiing exercises. They are specifically designed to stretch, to loosen, to prepare your body easily and naturally for the fluid rhythms of modern skiing.

THE EXERCISES

In all of the following exercises, the goal is relaxed stretching. Stand easily, comfortably, and breathe evenly and deeply. Perform each stretching movement up to the point of tension, but stop short of pain. If you feel pain, you are working against yourself; stop the exercise, or modify it to fit your own inelasticity, and then gradually work up to the full stretch.

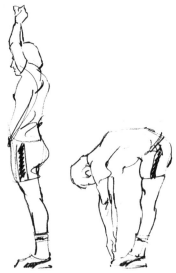

TOE TOUCHING. Relax into it. Stand straight, arms to side, knees locked. Now *roll* down, forward, curving the shoulders, letting the arms dangle and the head sink to the chest. Breathe deeply. Reach as far toward the toes as you can without bobbing. When your hamstring tendons feel the pull, relax in that position a few seconds. Remember to keep your neck relaxed.

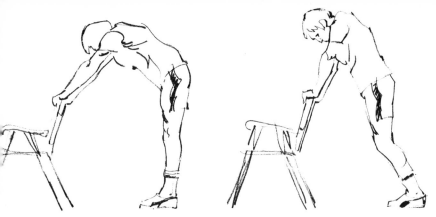

ANKLE BENDS. Use a chair or table for support. Stand facing the support, three or four feet from it, lean forward and place your hands on it. Keeping your heels on the floor, press forward and downward with your knees, until you feel the pull in your Achilles tendons. Stop short of pain. Proceed gently, gradually pressing your knees farther forward. Relax.

TORSO TWISTING. Stand comfortably, arms at side. Swing your arms loosely like a baseball swing, twisting your back, torso and rib cage. Twist until you feel the pull. Remember to breathe deeply. Alternate with *torso bends.*

15

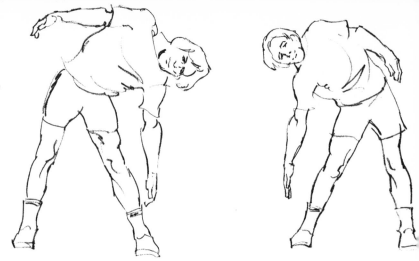

TORSO BENDS. Stand at a comfortable straddle. Keep torso and shoulders facing forward, and bend down as if to touch ankle on outside of your foot. Keep knees straight. Repeat on each side.

EDGING. Start in a sitting position, pressing weight against the outside of the foot, then the inside. Try the same thing standing, proceeding gently until you are sure the ankle will bear the weight of your body; then walk around for a few steps on the outsides of the feet, then the insides. Relax. This exercise is great for developing strong ankles for edge control.

SPLITS. Stand with the legs well apart, toes pointing outward at right angles to each other. Keeping most of your weight on one foot, with that knee straight, gradually bend the opposite knee until you feel pull along the "inseam" of the extended leg. Keep toes firmly on the floor. Reverse to the other leg. Relax. This develops snowplow muscles—and helps avoid a particularly wicked soreness.

TOE PULLS. Stand so you can support yourself at the side, with a chair, table or wall. Reach behind you and grab your toe, on the side away from the support. Pull your foot up toward your back, doubling your leg. Pull gently, until you feel the stretch in your thigh muscle as well as your foot. Relax as much as possible while pulling upwards. Change legs and repeat.

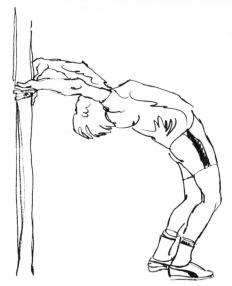

BACK BENDS. Stand three or four feet from a wall, and reach back over your head until you can touch the wall with your palms. Now "walk" your hands down the wall, gradually increasing the stretching force on your stomach muscles. If you've ever had back trouble, don't attempt this exercise until you've checked with your doctor.

NECK ROLLS. This is a great favorite with Yoga enthusiasts. Stand or sit in a relaxed position. Gently turn the head from side to side, as far as it will go without pain. Let it loll backward, then forward. Don't force. Roll the head gently around the periphery of its movement; then reverse direction. Make sure the shoulders are relaxed.

A PROGRAM

Muscles work by contracting. Most physical conditioning programs help develop the muscles' power to contract. But tight, tense muscles that never get extended to their full length will eventually lose some of their power to contract. Furthermore, the reaction of muscle tissue to pain, to fatigue—even to cold—is to contract. So the best possible program of preseason conditioning for skiing will combine stretching exercises with strength-building exercises so that the muscles are given a chance to extend to their full length before and after strength-building contracting exercises. This is especially necessary in conjunction with isometric exercises.

For maximum results, you should alternate stretching exercises with strength-building exercises that use the same sets of muscles. For example, you may want to start off your exercise program, after a warm-up, with knee bends. Follow them with the toe pulls from the preceding pages, to give the thigh muscles a chance to stretch back to full length. Similarly, follow push-ups—great for the lower back and stomach—with toe touching or back bends. Follow chinning with the gentle relaxation of neck rolls. And work over your lower extremities—with ankle bends, edging and splits—as you are resting from the more vigorous exercises. It's a good practice to follow jogging or other stamina-building regimes with a brief round of all the stretching exercises. The number of repetitions of each stretching exercise is up to you; since they are not tiring, just do them as long as you feel you are benefiting from them. And a good follow-up for the whole program is a short period of complete relaxation, flat on your back—the floor is the best place for it—to let the rest of the muscle groups relax completely.

2
The Equipment Revolution

THE INVENTION of the steel edge and the development of ski bindings that hold the boot securely to the ski were responsible for the first wave of the revolution in skiing, back in the 1930's. With those two developments, it was no longer necessary to be a super athlete to enjoy the sport. Now we are well into the second wave of that revolution. Development has been such that the modern ski boot allows immediate, micrometer-accurate movements of the feet and legs to be transmitted directly to the skis. Quick-reacting metal and plastic skis—lighter, stronger, shorter and redesigned in shape and curvature—can take those accurate movements and translate them into action on the snow. Improvements in bindings have assisted in the revolution, providing a secure clamp between boot and ski, yet providing a measure of safety by releasing in severe tumbles.

These developments have allowed more and more people to take up skiing and to progress quickly to a level of relative expertise that greatly increases their enjoyment of the sport.

Furthermore, the evolving modern equipment has changed the way people ski. Tyros advance beyond the laborious snowplow stage more quickly; intermediates find themselves progressing to graceful parallel skiing in days instead of weeks. The great majority of skiers turn more quickly and more frequently, ski under better control, and ski with more modern technique, thanks largely to improved equipment. The deep crouch, extreme forward lean and exaggerated rotation or counterrotation for powering turns have all just about disappeared from the slopes. Skiers with modern equipment can ski in a more upright, natural position, with less bodily contortion necessary to make the skis perform. Improved ski bottoms and flexing characteristics have reduced the amount of force needed to make skis turn, making possible development of whole new skiing techniques, such as *wedeln,* that fluid motion which makes the skier's legs operate almost like a whisk broom, the ski surfaces simply wiping back and forth across the snow. It's beautiful, it's fun and it isn't too hard to learn—*if* you have very good skis, and boots that support you rigidly enough so that when your legs make like a whisk broom your skis get the message. Accordingly, it's a good idea to know the basics about ski equipment before you select, either in the rental shop or at your local sports emporium.

Experts agree that the ski boot is the most important piece of equipment for successful, enjoyable skiing. The boot governs not only your ability to control your skis but also your comfort. The goal in ski boot design is absolute stiffness with regard to lateral movement. But stiffness-with-agony is just as unacceptable as a sloppy, uncontrollable boot. As a quick check to see whether a boot is suitable for you or not, look for these four key features:

1. With the boot on your foot, with thick wool socks on, you should be able, before the boot is fastened, to slide a finger down between your heel and the back of the boot. If you can't, the boot is too short.

2. With the boot fastened tightly, you should be able,

Boot should provide enough length to permit insertion of finger between heel and back of boot.

You should be able to bend your ankles enough to bring your knees forward of the toe of the boot.

Be sure there is room for further tightening of buckles, if boot material stretches during use.

with your feet flat on the floor, to bend your knees sufficiently to bring your knees forward of a vertical line from the toe of the boot. If you can't bend that far, the boot is too stiff for you. *But* if, when you bend forward, you see excessive bulging of the boot material in the angle of the ankle, the boot is not stiff enough.

3. With the boot fastened tightly, there should be a reasonable gap between the two sides of the closure, to give you room to tighten further when the leather stretches. (This check is not so critical with the new plastic boots, which stretch less or not at all.)

4. Check for pure comfort, and in particular for "hot spots"—areas of pressure which feel quite snug when you put the boot on but which can cause almost unbearable pain after an hour or so of hard use. Fortunately, most good boot shops can now custom-fit boots, by stretching and adjusting the boot material to any anomalies in the boot last or in your foot.

Ski selection is shrouded with mystique, principally because there are so many styles and models available that few people are familiar with all of them. A few generalizations are possible. A stiff ski tends to react more quickly and can be a little harder to turn; a soft ski is more forgiving but may feel dead to an experienced skier. All other things being equal, a longer ski will be harder to turn but more stable than a shorter one.

Years ago, whether you were a beginner or an expert, you skied on skis as much as fifteen inches longer than you were tall—and you'll still get that advice from some old-timers. But if you go to a good ski shop today, you'll probably be handed a pair almost the same length as your height. If you are heavy, strong, athletic, a quick learner, you can perhaps use a ski eight or ten inches longer than you are tall; if you are light in weight, timid, an absolute beginner or getting on in years, you can quite likely go to an even shorter length. Many ski schools today start beginners on very short skis, three or four feet long, and let the pupils work up in graduated stages to their proper ski length. This is known as the Graduated Length Method.

Ski bindings have advanced quite rapidly in recent years, but no binding can guarantee absolute safety. Whatever your choice of binding, it should be mounted on the ski by skilled personnel and adjusted to *your* boot before you venture onto the snow. You should understand how the binding is adjusted, how to fasten and release it, and how it releases in a fall. If you are not shown these things, ask about them. You should not "ski out" of your bindings— that is, they should not release during ordinary skiing maneuvers. But they should release in a hard fall, short of pain to your ankles or legs. If they don't, go back for an adjustment. It may save you more pain later.

The proper pole length is long enough to pass easily under your armpit when you are standing comfortably erect, in street shoes, on a hard floor. There is considerable controversy among hairsplitters about ski pole length these days. Remember that poles can easily be shortened, but they can't be lengthened. If you start with the recommended length, you can arrive at your own comfortable length as you progress as a skier.

The ski pole should pass easily under the armpit.

3
For Beginners Only

IN the bustle and rush of a popular ski area on a weekend, it's easy to get bulldozed into situations that can reduce the pleasure of your introduction to skiing. Take your time, and get yourself oriented. You'll get more skiing time, for instance, if you can arrange to get fitted for rental boots and skis the night before. If you don't, let the skiing time go in favor of better fitting. Linger over breakfast and let the bulk of the crowd get out of the rental shop, so the personnel can give you sufficient attention and so you can check your equipment thoroughly. (Your introduction will be that much more pleasant, of course, if you can make your first ski trip during an uncrowded midweek.)

Then head for ski school. There is no better advice for a beginner; you'll get personal attention and sound advice for dealing with the first clumsiness of having those long things fastened to your feet. If you're a little early for the start of lessons, so much the better; use the time to get accustomed to walking, turning around and—gently—sliding a bit. Don't

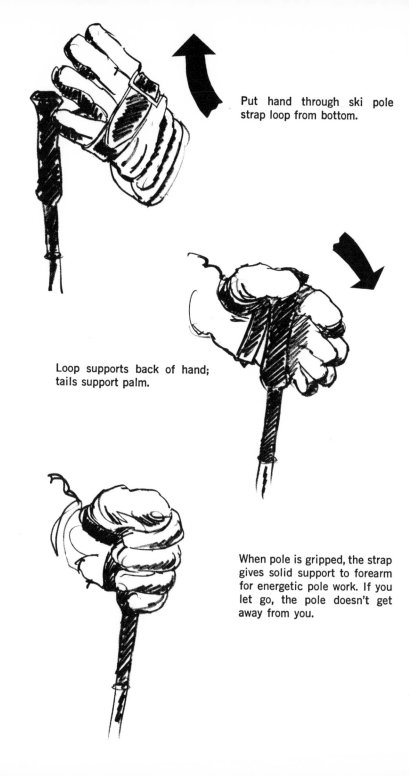

Put hand through ski pole strap loop from bottom.

Loop supports back of hand; tails support palm.

When pole is gripped, the strap gives solid support to forearm for energetic pole work. If you let go, the pole doesn't get away from you.

let the awkwardness of the skis freeze you, causing you to stand in immobilized fear. Hop up and down, swing your feet, walk from place to place, so you get accustomed to movement.

Similarly, get your bearings before you head for the ski hill. Find out where the ski school meets, where the beginners' areas are, where the smaller and slower lifts are. Ask questions. Don't be bashful—everyone is a beginner at least once. Get a map of the area, and compare it with what you can see. Pick gentle terrain, and stick to it; there's no more frustrating experience than getting to the top of a piece of scary-looking slope, without the ability or confidence to get yourself back down.

Some people are bothered by ski lifts; some never give them a second thought. If the process bothers you, watch for a while. Observe how the skiers sidestep into place; how, while they are waiting for the lift, they take their ski pole straps off their wrists, put both poles in the same hand (the hand opposite the vertical support of the lift) and look back over the opposite shoulder for the approaching lift device. Notice how they absorb the shock of the moving lift, by reaching back and taking the initial contact with the lift with their hands, and then guide their bodies into contact with the lift. It's really easy; if you are in doubt, tell the lift attendant. He'll gladly help.

Learn how to grasp your ski poles correctly: hand up through the strap from the bottom, then grasping the handle with the straps underneath the fist, supporting the arm. Learn how to keep track of your skis when you carry them on your shoulder, bottoms together, turned-up tips forward. Learn to watch for the tails over your shoulder, as you turn—so you scalp fewer innocent bystanders. Learn to climb: sidestepping, with skis parallel across the fall line (the steepest line down the slope, that a snowball would follow if it were allowed to roll down the hill); or herringbone, as illustrated, to give you a first introduction to edge control. And learn to do kick turns—they'll help you out of tight places.

The herringbone climb. Start with short steps, pushing your knees forward to set inside edges of your skis and give you purchase on snow. Keep your poles outside the V of your skis; push off with them. If you get tired on a long climb, alternate herringbone with sidestepping.

And, reading this book, begin to pick up some of the terms, like "fall line" and "herringbone." The reason isn't so you can make sophisticated cocktail talk (although that's allowed) but so you can communicate with your instructor, describe your troubles and understand his advice.

Now—go to ski school. And look for the pin on the instructor's sweater or parka that specifies that he is a certified professional ski instructor.

To do a kick turn, Billy Kidd stands facing slightly downhill, his uphill ski pole planted near the tips of his skis for support, his downhill pole well back toward the tails of his skis. (A). He swings his downhill ski forward and up,

A

B

until its tail rests on snow (B). Next he swings the ski around to reverse direction, pivoting the ski on its tail (C), places it firmly across the fall line and puts weight on it (D), setting the uphill edge so it will hold him in place. Then he swings the uphill ski around easily, plants it parallel to the first ski moved, shifts weight fully, planting both uphill edges, and moves his poles around to support him in the new direction (E).

C

D

E

If you fall and have trouble getting up, try this: Swing both skis parallel, directly across the fall line, so you can set the uphill edges; that way you won't slip back down when you try to stand. Grasp both poles together, place one hand near the baskets for steadiness, then reach up with the other hand, grab the poles at the handles and haul yourself upright.

4
The Basics

SKIING is a way of sliding down hills on snow. So are sledding, tobogganing, and several other minor wintertime sports, but none of the others has captured the public imagination as skiing has, nor attracted the number of devotees. The difference is control. Skiing adds a whole new element to the pleasure of zipping down an inclined surface: absolute control, enabling you to go where you want, avoid terrain that you want to avoid, stop and start over again whenever you want, and vary your rate of speed. Control, in skiing, is everything.

Since a skier *turns* to guide his course, to control his speed, and even to stop, attention has been focused on turning to the virtual exclusion of everything else. "Turning is what it's all about," one ski editor once remarked; "everything else is persiflage." The sentiment is not quite accurate —that persiflage includes such basics as balance and equilibrium. Before you become obsessed with carving perfect turns, it pays to spend a little time on these basics. The better you master them, the easier you'll find it to perfect your turning later.

BALANCE AND STANCE

Your best stance on your skis is simply one which keeps you balanced, ready to react to any change of terrain or snow conditions. To find that position, stand with your skis about as far apart as the width of your hips and rock your weight gently back and forth until you find the stance in which you feel ready for anything. You won't want to try to ski standing at attention; you also don't need to crouch over your skis like a charging lineman. You'll find yourself most comfortable, and best prepared for action, with your weight on the balls of your feet and your knees, ankles and waist all slightly bent. By bending, you lower your center of gravity, which makes you more stable. You also prepare the three basic hinges of the body—knees, ankles and waist —to absorb shock, to react quickly by shifting body weight,

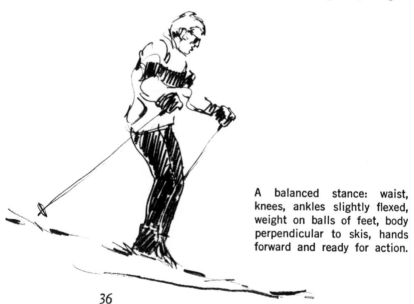

A balanced stance: waist, knees, ankles slightly flexed, weight on balls of feet, body perpendicular to skis, hands forward and ready for action.

and to initiate any of the required moves of skiing. Some skiers find it helpful to bend their knees and ankles until they are conscious of pressure from their boot tops on the front of their ankles—and then they try to keep that pressure there continually, as a reminder to keep their ankles and knees bent while they are skiing. Whatever memory aids you use, find a way to stand that feels securely balanced, which you can maintain without undue strain on any single set of muscles, and from which you can react in any direction. Don't think of this stance as a *position* so much as a way of preparing your body for action, a fluid state that keeps you ready for anything.

Exercises for Balance

1. Choose a gentle beginners' slope with dips and bumps in it. Schuss the slope (make a straight run down it) over the bumps, absorbing terrain changes by flexing at knees, ankles and waist. Be ready to shift weight forward or back to adjust to changes of attitude of skis and changing snow conditions. You'll find if you press with your toes, as if to hold the tips of the skis more securely on the ground, the ski tips will follow the bumps better and you'll feel less apt to be thrown in the air.

A

Billy Kidd absorbs a bump. In Figure A he's in a balanced stance, running straight down the fall line, flexed and ready for action.

As skis run up over bump (B), Billy moves weight forward and lets body hinge loosely at knees, hips and ankles, so upper body is relatively unaffected by change of attitude.

B

Coming down back side of the bump (C), he consciously presses toes downward, to keep fronts of skis in contact with snow, and lets body "unhinge" to keep his stable position.

C

38

2. Experiment, while straight running, with changes of stance. Lift the tail of one ski, then the other. Hop the tails of both skis off the ground simultaneously, as you go. Skate. There is no better familiarization exercise than skating. Concentrate on keeping your body relaxed, your position comfortable. Look where you are going. Relax—have fun.

On the flat, Billy Kidd practices hopping tails of skis. He plants both poles for stability, springs lightly up and forward, leaving ski tips on snow but hopping tails from side to side. This is invaluable practice for controlling skis in quick work; you should learn to hop tails back and forth rapidly with good control.

39

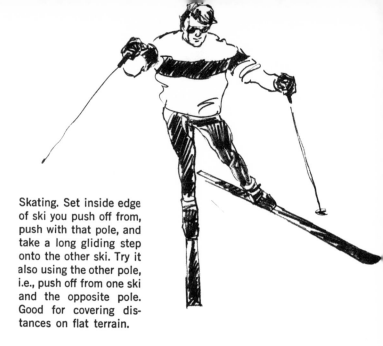

Skating. Set inside edge of ski you push off from, push with that pole, and take a long gliding step onto the other ski. Try it also using the other pole, i.e., push off from one ski and the opposite pole. Good for covering distances on flat terrain.

EDGE CONTROL

The advantage of the modern ski boot is that it enables you to transmit delicate movements of your feet and legs directly to your skis, without waste motion. The reason you need to transmit those delicate movements is in order to control your ski edges. Your edges are your steering wheel and your brakes—they are the principal source of guidance. They provide your grip on the snow when you want grip, and they carve your turns. You must be in command of them.

Stand comfortably on your skis on flat terrain, and push both knees to one side or the other; you'll rock the skis slightly and push one edge of each ski into the snow. Stand across the fall line on a slope and you'll find that, just by standing, you are pushing your uphill edges into the snow—edging. You'll also find that the way you are accomplishing this edging is by pushing the knees toward the hill. Be sure to push your knees together simultaneously; otherwise you'll edge your skis unequally, which will lead to problems later.

Billy Kidd pushes his knees toward the hill to set his uphill edges. Experiment first on flat terrain, pushing the knees to one side and then the other to set right and left edges alternately.

If the slope is steep you will need to push not only your knees but also your hips toward the hill, in order to cant the soles of your skis sufficiently to grip the snow. To do so successfully, you'll have to lean away from the hill with your upper body. There is a natural tendency to lean in toward the slope, to seek the security of closer contact with the ground, but to do so will cause the edges to slip out of contact with the snow and you'll fall. You must lean away from the hill in order to keep weight on your uphill edges. This canting of the upper body in order to increase edging is called *angulation*; sometimes the basic position, with knees and hips pushed toward the hill and upper body leaned outward, is referred to as the "comma" position, because of the commalike curve of the body.

Here, Billy exaggerates angulation to show extreme comma position for very steep slopes. Knees and hips are pushed toward the slope, upper body curved outward to keep weight over edges, edges firmly set.

SIDESLIPPING

Now, experiment a bit with edge control. Your edges are set into the hill. Reduce the push of your knees toward the hill, reduce the amount your hips are pushed toward the uphill side, and you will start sliding sideways downhill. Your edges are released. Push your knees back toward the hill, and you'll slow and stop. By rolling the knees from side to side, pushing them alternately away from and toward the slope, you'll find you can work your way down the slope in short, gentle sideslips. Practice releasing and resetting your

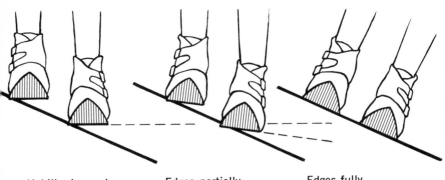

Uphill edges set.

Edges partially released. Sideslip starts—gently.

Edges fully released.

edges until you can start, stop, slow and speed up your sideslipping at will. If you have trouble getting started, push off with your poles on the uphill side; if the motion bothers you at first, plant one pole downhill from your skis and sideslip into it, using it to keep your skis from running away. Master the sideslip; it will, in an emergency, get you down any slope—and you'll use the skills you learn in sideslipping in every bit of skiing you ever do.

In practicing sideslipping, Billy Kidd plants his downhill pole for stability, and then, by alternately pushing his knees into the hill and letting them come back, he sideslips gently down the hill. Once you've got this, practice without the downhill pole, on steeper slopes. Later, when you come to a slope that is steeper than you want to ski, you can sideslip down to more enjoyable terrain.

43

Exercise for Sideslipping

Release your edges and, as you begin sideslipping, shift your weight forward toward the tips of your skis. You will begin to sideslip at an angle, with forward motion as well as sideways motion. Reverse the procedure, shifting the weight to the rear, and you'll slide to the rear as well as down. Practice until you can do both, stopping and starting the motion in either direction by releasing and resetting the edges and by moving weight forward and backward on the skis. Remember to keep loose, knees bent, weight out from the hill.

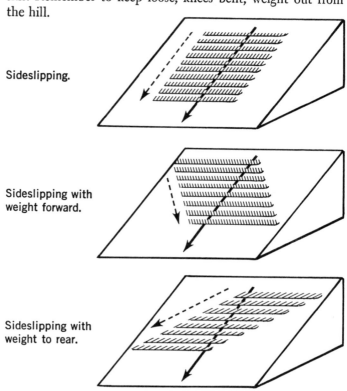

Sideslipping.

Sideslipping with weight forward.

Sideslipping with weight to rear.

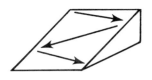

TRAVERSING

The basic method of coming down a hill is by a long series of diagonal runs across the hill, with turns at each end. The diagonal runs between turns are called *traverses*. Straight down the fall line leads to too much speed, so you begin by running across the hill, gradually increasing the angle as you become able to handle more speed.

Traversing is a much neglected art. It develops balance and edge control and, as the initiating point for all turns, must be stable and in control. To traverse in a straight line, stand across the fall line, with skis a comfortable distance apart, the uphill ski advanced about half a boot length ahead of the lower ski. Your knees are pushed toward the hill, to set your edges, and your upper body leans outward, away from the hill. Put a little more weight on the lower ski than on the upper. Push off. Remember to keep loose, in your balanced stance. You may be more comfortable with your shoulders turned slightly toward the valley. The American Ski Technique specifies that knees, ankles, hips and shoulders are parallel. With the uphill ski advanced (which helps prevent your ski tips from crossing), this will face you slightly downhill.

Billy Kidd traverses—uphill ski slightly ahead, downhill ski carrying more weight, knees pushed subtly into the hill. For better balance at first, keep skis a few inches apart.

In a traverse, your balanced stance comes fully into play. As the terrain changes or the snow conditions vary, you will need to shift weight forward or backward to compensate for the changes in speed. On gentle slopes, you'll feel more comfortable with your skis farther apart; on steep slopes you'll want to bring them closer together. You will need to react, respond, while keeping your skis pointed in the angle of traverse you want to run and while keeping your weight on your downhill ski. (If you put too much weight on the uphill ski, you'll begin to turn downhill.)

Exercises for Traversing

1. Practice traversing varied terrain, over bumps, on both steep and gentle slopes. Note that to get more grip—for steeper slopes or icier snow conditions—you push the knees toward the slope and lean the upper body farther away from the slope.

2. To develop balance, try lifting your uphill ski off the snow as you traverse. Begin by lifting just the tail of the ski; when you are comfortable doing that, lift the entire ski, traversing on just the downhill ski.

3. While in a slow, gentle traverse, release your edges slightly by letting your knees push out slightly, away from the hill. You'll start sideslipping as you travel forward, increasing your angle of descent without increasing your speed. Set your edges again by pushing knees toward the slope, and you'll resume the traverse angle. Practice stopping and starting the sideslip as you make long traverses across the slope.

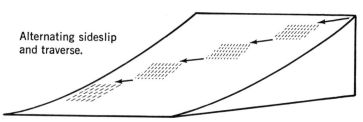

Alternating sideslip and traverse.

THE SNOWPLOW

There is one other technique for getting down a hill before you have any great amount of experience in ski technique—the snowplow. It is particularly effective in controlling your speed in your first turns through the fall line, and it will also help you stop in close quarters, when you haven't room to maneuver.

The secret to snowplowing is edge control, just as it is in traversing and sideslipping. In those exercises, however, you edged your skis together, in the same direction. In the snowplow you edge them separately, in opposition to each other.

To edge your skis, you have learned to push the knee in the direction you want the ski edged. To snowplow, you are going to use the inside edges of both skis, and you can't push both knees to the inside unless your legs are spread. Push the tails of your skis outward so they make a V, the tips four or five inches apart. Keep you knees bent slightly. By varying the amount of knee push inward, you control the amount of edging. To increase speed, decrease the angle formed by your skis and let up on the pressure on the inside edges; to decrease speed or stop, increase the angle between your skis and increase the pressure on the inside edges.

You must put pressure on the edges equally; if you don't, the tips will try to cross or you'll tend to do a split. You must also keep your weight equalized between the skis to achieve a stable snowplow. Strive to keep your body upright, balanced over your skis. If your skis tend to separate, you are probably sitting back too far; if you feel as if you are going to fall over the tips, you are edging too much, or bending forward too much at the waist.

Exercises for Snowplow

1. Pick a gentle slope, start directly down the fall line,

and begin snowplowing. As you go down the slope, bring the ski tails back together, then push them apart again, brushing the tails in and out of the snowplow as you go, feeling the amount of edging necessary to control speed and maintain stability.

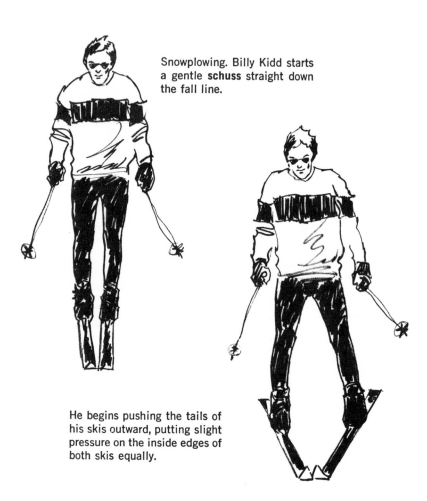

Snowplowing. Billy Kidd starts a gentle **schuss** straight down the fall line.

He begins pushing the tails of his skis outward, putting slight pressure on the inside edges of both skis equally.

2. Once you feel comfortable and stable in your snowplow, try this variation. Pick a gentle slope, as before, and start down the fall line, snowplowing. Increase the pressure inward on your right knee, to increase edging, while letting up pressure on the left knee. You will begin traveling on a bias, veering toward the left. Increase the pressure inward on that knee and let up on the right; you will change direction and begin veering to the right. Practice both until you get a good feel for the control of your edges, and the effect of edging on your snowplow.

In a full snowplow, Billy can control his speed—or stop—by pushing his knees forward and down to increase the angle of the inside edges of his skis.

5
The First Turns

SNOWPLOW TURN

THE snowplow turn is primarily an exercise for teaching how the skis work in a turn and where body weight must be placed. It also gives you further practice in edge control, albeit separate edge control. Don't fixate on the snowplow turn; learn it, observe it, learn what you can from it and go on to more advanced—and more satisfying—turns.

Snowplow down a gentle beginners' slope, skis evenly edged, your weight equally divided between your skis. Now bring your right shoulder slightly back, and lean your weight onto your right ski. You will start to turn to your left. If you keep your weight over your right ski, you will turn until you are at a right angle to the fall line and then stop. Try another, this time putting weight on the left ski, to turn to the right.

Billy Kidd starts his snowplow down a gentle slope, weight evenly distributed.

To turn to his left, he bends right knee, puts weight on that ski, pushes right knee in direction he wants to turn.

Turning away from the fall line, Billy straightens up, equalizes pressure on edges and stops.

Exercises for Snowplow Turns

1. As a memory aid, think of the knee as a means of steering the snowplow turn. If you want to turn left, you put your weight on your right ski. If you concentrate on bending that knee, pushing with it in the direction you want to turn, you will ensure that your weight is transferred to the proper ski and that it is properly edged. You will also be sure not to stiffen your downhill knee, a common bad habit of beginners.

2. Link your snowplow turns, making an S-shaped track down the slope. Control your speed by increasing or decreasing edging—by varying pressure toward the center of the turn with the knees—and by increasing or decreasing the angle between your skis. Don't complete turns, but, after turning a few degrees off the fall line, shift your weight smoothly to your uphill ski, push inward with that knee and start another turn back through the fall line.

CHRISTIE INTO THE HILL

In your sideslipping exercises, when you varied your weight placement on your skis and let them slip forward as well as sideways, you were beginning to experiment with a rudimentary form of the christie into the hill, or christie uphill. You were changing your direction while your skis were parallel. Now we go a step further and learn more about control.

From a gentle traverse, increase the bend at your knees, ankles and waist with a light sinking motion, and then come back up, releasing your edges and moving your weight forward as you do. The tails of your skis will start to slip downhill, and you will turn uphill. Stop the turning motion by re-edging, pushing your knees and hips toward the hill, and by sinking slightly again. Remember this down-up-down motion with your body; you'll be using it more later. Sideslip back to your original line and continue your traverse.

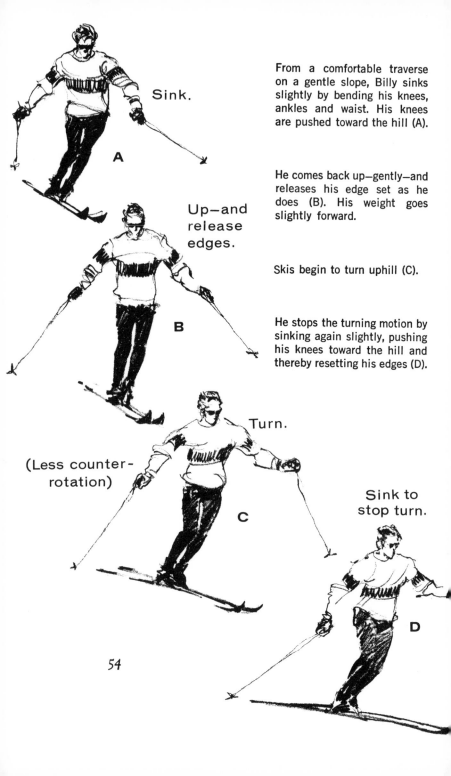

Sink.

A

From a comfortable traverse on a gentle slope, Billy sinks slightly by bending his knees, ankles and waist. His knees are pushed toward the hill (A).

Up—and release edges.

B

He comes back up—gently—and releases his edge set as he does (B). His weight goes slightly forward.

Skis begin to turn uphill (C).

He stops the turning motion by sinking again slightly, pushing his knees toward the hill and thereby resetting his edges (D).

(Less counter-rotation)

Turn.

C

Sink to stop turn.

D

Exercises for Christie into the Hill

1. To accustom yourself to unweighting your skis, practice, on a long traverse, the slow sink and gentle rise that will momentarily unweight the ski bottoms. You may find you begin to turn uphill *without* releasing your edges, which indicates you need to pay more attention to edge control: knees pushed toward the hill, upper body leaned away from it. Remember to keep the downhill knee bent; if you lock it, you will lean into the hill.

2. Try christies into the hill with and without counterrotation (reversed shoulder, or pulling the downhill shoulder back as you turn—see page 61). You may find one more comfortable or more successful than the other. The primary purpose of counterrotation, in this case, is to force you to keep weight on the downhill ski until you want to release its edge. You may not need it.

STEM TURN

Learning to ski should be a natural progression from one exercise to another, gradually increasing in speed, grace and sureness. If you have mastered the uphill christie and the linked snowplow turns, you are ready to learn the first of the natural, flowing turns by which you can link traverses and work your way smoothly from the top of the slope to the bottom. The stem turn is an intermediate step, but it allows you to handle a little more speed than the snowplow, and to turn a little more gracefully. Many skiers find that with it and its close cousin, the stem christie, they have all the skiing technique they need to get ample pleasure out of the sport.

The stem turn will accustom you to a more rapid weight shift than linked snowplow turns. When you did linked snowplow turns, you spread your skis in a V and then swung

C

D

E

F

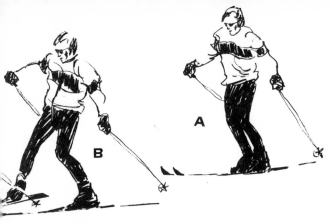

From a comfortable traverse (A), Billy Kidd prepares to make a stem turn to the left. He pushes his uphill ski outward (B), as if to form half a snowplow. Billy begins to shift his weight onto his uphill ski (C). In Figure D, he has shifted his upper body to weight the uphill ski—the outside ski of the turn—more heavily. He is beginning to put edging pressure on the inside edge of that ski. Billy has turned across the fall line (E). He is pushing the knee of his right leg toward the inside of the turn, to increase edging pressure and steer the turn to a new traverse. Finishing the turn (F), Billy is bringing the inside ski alongside the other and beginning to equalize weight. Billy has completed the turn (G). Weight is on the inside edge of the downhill ski. In Figure H, Billy begins the new traverse, knees pushed toward the hill, his uphill ski weighted only slightly, ready to be stemmed outward for a turn in the other direction.

your weight back and forth, over one ski and then the other, in order to turn. In the stem turn you will actually step your weight onto the outside ski of the turn.

From a comfortable traverse, weight on downhill ski, push the tail of your uphill ski outward, as if to form half a snowplow. This ski now points in the direction you want to turn, toward the fall line. Now shift your weight smoothly to the uphill ski, stepping onto it, and, as in the snowplow, lean your upper body over the outside ski. Keep that outside knee bent and push it in and downhill, in the direction you want to turn. As you come around the turn, let your skis run back to a parallel position, and resume your traverse in the new direction. Note that by putting your weight on your outside ski during the turn and keeping it there, your weight is already on the proper ski—now the downhill one—for the new traverse. Your uphill ski, with less weight on it, is ready to be stemmed for the next turn, in the opposite direction.

You should begin your stem turn with a little more speed than you carried into your snowplow turns. On your first turns across the fall line, you may feel that you are in danger of going out of control, with too much speed; remember that as you come around to the fall line, you are in a narrow snowplow and can control your speed just as you did in the snowplow, by increasing the angle between your skis— pushing the tails out farther—and by edging more—pushing your knees toward each other and forward.

Exercises for the Stem Turn

1. Practice the stem turn movements while standing still on a flat surface, with or without skis. (You can even do this in your living room.) From an imaginary traverse, with your weight on your downhill ski, step your uphill ski out into a half snowplow. Shift your weight onto it smoothly, lean over it, push that knee in to edge the stemmed ski,

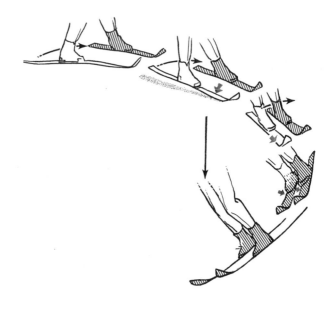

Darkened area shows where preponderance of weight is placed during a stem turn to the right. As the uphill ski is stemmed, weight goes to that ski, remains there during turn, then is gradually shifted back to equal weighting as turn is finished.

then bring the other ski alongside. Notice the necessary edge changes.

2. On a long, very gentle slope, one you can schuss without fear, head straight down the fall line. As you go, push the tail of one ski outward in a stem, let it run back alongside the other, then push the other out into a stem. Gradually begin shifting a little weight onto the stemmed ski as you keep repeating the exercise, until you are making a subtle S track down the hill—and are in fact linking stem turns through the fall line.

SQUARE VS. REVERSED SHOULDER

So far, you've been advised that you *may* want to pull your downhill shoulder back on traverses and pull your outside shoulder back on stem and snowplow turns. The American Ski Technique specifies that this shoulder *should* be pulled back slightly. You may be confused by conflicting instructions.

Ski teaching methods change, just as skiing styles change. Years ago, skiers were taught to initiate turns with a powerful rotation of the shoulders in the direction of the turn. Then the idea of counterrotation swept most of the ski world, decreeing that skiers initiate turns by a sharp counterrotation of the shoulders and upper body. More recently the trend is toward a squared-up stance, the shoulders carried at right angles to the skis.

The winds of change sometimes make a tempest in a teapot. As skis have become easier to turn, ski slopes have generally become smoother and better groomed, and ski boots have been stiffened, it has become considerably easier to learn to turn skis. It is no longer necessary for the skier to generate great bursts of muscle power in order to get his turns started. You can learn to ski with any of the three styles: rotation, counterrotation or squared shoulders. Don't worry about which is most stylish; find out which works best for you.

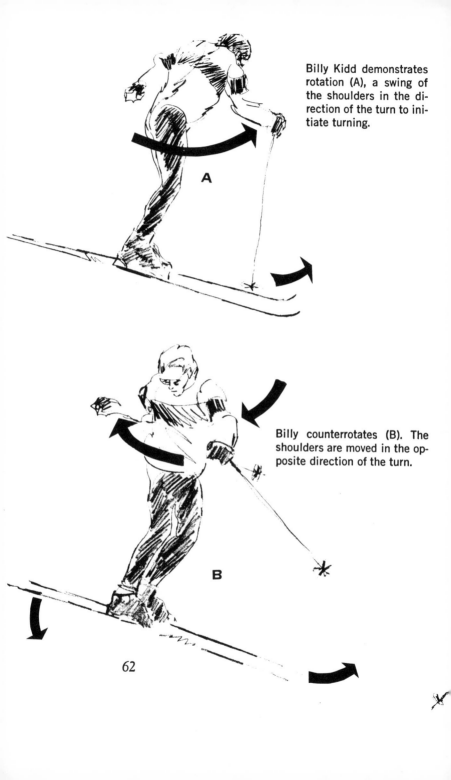

Billy Kidd demonstrates rotation (A), a swing of the shoulders in the direction of the turn to initiate turning.

A

Billy counterrotates (B). The shoulders are moved in the opposite direction of the turn.

B

As it happens, several elements of the reversed-shoulder counterrotating technique have proved to be handy aids for beginners—that's why the American Ski Technique uses them. Carrying the downhill shoulder slightly back helps remind you to keep your upper body leaned away from the hill. Pulling your outside shoulder back on turns helps you to remember to keep your weight on the outside ski of the turn.

We'll have more to say about style in a later chapter, but for now, experiment. When you get an exercise down pat, vary your body angulation and shoulder position. Don't freeze into one body position and refuse to abandon it. Stay loose. You may find a way of performing the exercise that is easier for you, that makes you more effective as a skier. You'll also be on the way to developing your own personal style of skiing. The easiest way for you will be the most natural and, in the end, the most graceful.

HOW A SKI TURNS

Sometimes it seems that those long boards that are skis won't turn at all, that it is somehow unnatural to expect this of something so straight and stiff. It may help you to understand just how the physical object that is a ski *can* turn, irrespective of whatever physical gyrations you may be performing on it.

C

The squared position lends itself to modern ski styles, in which the upper body is generally quiet while the legs do most of the work.

63

A ski is *not* a straight, stiff object. It is subtly curved in two distinct ways. Place a ski flat on the floor, and you will see that it makes contact at only two places, the tail and a midpoint near the turned-up nose. Place it on its edge on the floor, or sight down the side of the ski, and you will see that that dimension is also curved; the ski is widest, again, at a point near the turned-up nose and at the tail.

Side Cut.

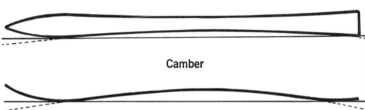

Camber

Cut a stiff piece of paper so that its edge makes a gentle arc, simulating the curved *side cut* of a ski. Now, tilt that cardboard until the curve of its arc makes contact with a flat surface along its entire length, and envision the track it would make if you slid it along the surface while maintaining that contact. The track would be a circle, corresponding to the arc you've cut in the paper.

Now, envision the curved side of a ski being edged into an inclined snow surface. If you edge the uphill side, the ski will seek a path maintaining its angle on the surface. If you swing toward the downhill edge, the ski will follow the natural curve of its own side cut, or arc. (In the transition, when no edge is set, the ski will simply slide sideways on its flat bottom—sideslipping.)

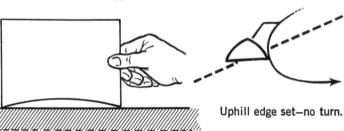

Uphill edge set—no turn.

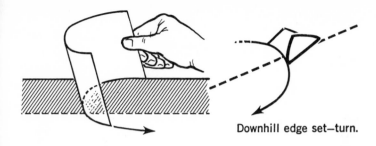

Downhill edge set—turn.

Similarly, the curve of the bottom of the ski, called the *camber,* serves indirectly to aid turning. Its purpose is to distribute the weight of the skier evenly. Without it the skier's weight would be concentrated directly under the feet; with the weight distributed evenly, the side cut can come into contact with the snow along its full length, when the ski is edged, and thus can function as an arc.

THE STEM CHRISTIE

So far the turning you've done has been somewhat passive. You have put the skis in certain positions, shifted your weight according to instructions, and your skis have done the turning for you. In effect, the skis have turned you. Now you are going to make the transition to the active phase of skiing, in which *you* turn the skis, *you* control them, and skiing becomes an active, exhilarating sport of infinite subtlety.

As a transition step between these active and passive phases, you should practice stem christies, which combine the stem turn and the christie into the hill. The stem christie gives you a stable and reassuring base from which to start and allows you to begin learning more about working your skis together. To do a stem christie, you begin a stem turn, but as you start to turn into the fall line, you bring your skis parallel and christie into the hill to finish the turn. Take it step by step.

You are in a comfortable traverse. You push the tail of the uphill ski out, forming half a snowplow. As you begin to

Billy Kidd begins a stem christie to the right from a comfortable traverse (A).

He sinks slightly by bending his knees, plants his right ski pole for balance and rhythm, and stems his uphill ski (B).

He rises slightly as he begins the weight shift to the stemmed uphill ski (C). As he steps off the downhill ski, he releases his edges as in a christie into the hill and brings his lower, downhill ski parallel to the stemmed uphill ski.

Headed almost into the fall line (D), Billy's weight is up and forward; his edges are released. His skis are turning rapidly now.

He completes his stem christie by sinking again, setting his edges (E). If his skis had a tendency to turn too much at this point, he would push knees and hips toward the slope for a more emphatic edge set.

Billy resumes a secure and comfortable traverse (F), ready to start another stem christie in the other direction.

C

D

E

F

transfer weight onto that ski, you begin turning into the fall line. As you do, bring the inside ski parallel to the outside one, rising slightly to do so and releasing your edges. You are now starting your christie into the hill. Your edges are released; your weight is slightly forward. As your skis come around, you push your knees in toward the hill and angulate your upper body away from the hill, to set your "new" uphill edges and stop your turn. You are now in a traverse in the opposite direction from the way you started.

Your goal now is to reduce the amount of stem necessary to get you properly launched into your turn and to increase the proportion of the turn that you make with the skis parallel. You can begin to work toward this goal in a number of ways, in the following exercises.

Exercises for the Stem Christie

1. Practice the movements on the flat, standing in place. Step out into a stem, transfer weight with an upward motion of the body, release edges and bring skis parallel simultaneously. Reset edges for the imaginary opposite traverse.

2. Practice christies into the hill. You must be smoothly proficient at this exercise to avoid a feeling of panic as you turn into the fall line with your skis together. Do christies into the hill from a schuss, gradually increasing speed, so that you can use the uphill christie as a means of stopping.

3. Try stem christies with reverse shoulder. Your uphill shoulder is slightly forward during your traverse. As you transfer weight to the uphill ski and release your edges, pull your uphill (outside in the coming turn) shoulder back farther, to give you a correct lead in the new traverse. This will help you remember where to keep your weight.

4. Exaggerate. As you stem the uphill ski, increase the bend at the knee and waist, for a sinking motion; as you transfer weight to the stemmed ski and release your edges, do so with a pronounced up movement, which will help you

pull your inside ski parallel with the stemmed ski. As you finish the turn, sink back down, to help set the edges for the new traverse.

STEM CHRISTIE WITH A DOWNHILL STEM

Stemming the downhill ski to initiate a stem christie has been in disfavor among American ski instructors for several years, but the Europeans have recently readopted it as a teaching technique. You may want to try it. The downhill stem christie is done approximately as the uphill stem is done, except that the downhill ski, when stemmed, gives you a more secure platform from which to launch the new turn. The stemmed ski becomes a secure base, from which you step off into the christie portion of the turn.

HOW CLOSE TOGETHER?

Some skiers look as if they were skiing on a single ski, simply because they've trained themselves to ski with their legs and skis very close together. The goal of the super stylists seems to be to ski as though both legs were stuffed into one pant leg. Such skiing is beautiful to watch.

It's difficult to learn, though, particularly if you try to emulate those skiers too early in the learning process. The learning skier needs stability more than style. You don't achieve stability by narrowing your base. Forget, for now, about keeping your legs and skis absolutely nailed together; concentrate instead on learning to move your skis simultaneously. You'll learn faster.

A handy indicator of your own particular needs, for stability, is the width of your hips. Keep your skis under your hip sockets, and you'll have stability without sacrificing flexibility or getting in such awkward positions that you can't react to the terrain. Some of our best racers ski this way; they do so in order to be able to step higher for a better line on a gate, or to skate in order to accelerate.

Certain conditions call for a wider stance, such as schussing on fairly flat slopes that are rutted. Others, such as very steep slopes or deep unpacked snow, can be handled more successfully with the skis closer together.

To stop the turning motion, Billy sinks slightly, pushes his knees subtly toward the hill, and brings his upper body out away from the hill (F). This sets his edges and gives him a stable platform for the next turn.

The point is to find the relationship that makes you feel most comfortable and most stable. You can be sure of one thing—if the racers do it, there's no shame attached to "wide-tracking" for stability.

From a steep traverse, Billy Kidd begins a stem christie to the left with the downhill ski stemmed (A).

Billy's weight is primarily on his uphill ski (B). He begins to stem the downhill ski into a half snowplow.

Billy then transfers his weight to the stemmed ski, sets the inside edge hard, and reaches forward to plant his ski pole (C).

Billy "bounces" off his downhill stem; with relatively little weight on either ski, he begins to turn and to bring his skis back together simultaneously (D).

Then, his stem closed, he completes his turn with skis loosely parallel (E).

71

6
Christies

THE christie, or parallel turn, is the fundamental building block of expert skiing. Before you can make parallel turns, all your skiing efforts are aimed at mastering that one flowing maneuver. Once you've mastered it, the entire world of skiing excitement opens up before you. "Expert" is, of course, a relative term, but if you can do a parallel turn you will be put in the expert level of ski school classes—and then you begin learning pure subtleties.

Parallel skiing doesn't mean skiing with the skis touching each other, but it does mean that maneuvers are initiated and carried out with the two skis pointing in the same direction; the skis do not "open" and "close" as an aid to making turns.

You've already done christies into the hill; now you are going to initiate the same christie from a traverse and carry it through the fall line into a new traverse. To do so, you will have to pay a little more attention to getting a good beginning—i.e., initiating your turn from a traverse position that is stable enough to allow you to unweight your skis effectively. You'll have to perform the unweighting a little more distinctly at first, until you get accustomed to moving the skis together. And you'll have to keep practicing the edge release and control that will allow you to let your skis slip when you want them to and hold when you need firm control. Take it step by step.

You are in a comfortable traverse. You sink slightly to set your edges securely and prepare yourself to unweight. You spring lightly forward and upward to unweight. You transfer your weight to your outside ski—the uphill one, at the initiation of the turn—and release your edges. This allows your skis to begin turning. As you come to the fall line, you push your knees toward the center of the turn, allowing your weight to transfer to the outside ski of the turn and your upper body to lean outward. You also push the inside ski slightly forward, so it will be in the lead once the turn is completed. As your skis come around to finish the turn, you sink again at waist, hips and knees, pushing your knees toward the uphill ski to set the edges and stop the turning motion. Your weight is away from the hill, your uphill ski is in the lead, your uphill edges are set; you resume a traverse in the opposite direction.

To reduce the seeming complexity of all these motions, go through this drill on dry land. Stand with your feet a few inches apart, one foot a half length ahead of the other. Rise up on your toes and pivot both feet, settling down again facing in the opposite direction, with the other foot now a half length ahead. Now repeat, this time imagining yourself on skis in a traverse, your uphill edges set. As you rise on your toes you are unweighting; as you pivot, you are releasing your edges and turning your skis; as you come down facing in the opposite direction, you are resetting your opposite edges for the new traverse. Put in a little angulation of the upper body and knee push to set your edges, and you've got a good dry-land drill for learning to coordinate the movements of a parallel turn on skis.

74

Remember, for every turn you must do the following things: (1) unweight your skis, (2) start your skis turning and (3) release your edges as you start turning and then set your opposite edges to stop your turn and control your new traverse. As we will see, there are several ways to accomplish each of these steps.

UNWEIGHTING

Any movement that momentarily reduces the weight on the skis, or the length of ski in contact with the snow, will serve to allow you to initiate a turn. You can sneak unweighting by using your momentum and bumps in the terrain; you will find turns easier if you allow even a small bump to propel you momentarily and subtly upward and then initiate your turn with this lift. But you will want to be able to turn anywhere, without waiting for bumps to come along, so it pays to learn to unweight yourself properly.

Ski instructors talk about "up unweighting" and "down unweighting." To up unweight, you crouch or sink slightly on your skis and then spring lightly upward and forward. To down unweight, you quickly pull your legs upward underneath you, sinking quickly, leaving the bulk of your body mass momentarily unweighted. Either method is in reality a subtle jump; either will reduce the weight on your skis sufficiently to allow you to turn them. As a rule, up unweighting, with its more pronounced and slower movements, is easier to learn as a starter. It gives you more time to get the other parts of the turn under way. Later you'll find that down unweighting is quicker and more efficient for certain types of terrain and snow conditions.

Note that reducing the amount of the ski in contact with the snow can also serve as a kind of unweighting. You'll find that as you ride over a bump, even if your weight isn't propelled into the air, the reduced contact patch of ski with snow, while you are on top of the bump, will allow you

Billy Kidd prepares for the classic parallel turn. He starts with a sinking motion—exaggerated here for clarity—and reaches out with his ski pole to trigger the turn (A). Billy has already begun to rise (B), his knees straightening, his weight coming up, forward, and off his skis. The mystical moment in parallel skiing (C): With racer efficiency, Billy has released his uphill edges, begun to transfer his weight to the outside ski of the turn, and started his skis turning. The turning force comes from a subtle combination of movements—in this case, primarily a steering movement with the feet and knees, in combination with released edges. With his weight on the outside ski of the turn (D), Billy is beginning to push his knees in toward the center of the turn, to provide control of the turning radius with the inside edges. Without this controlling movement, his skis would turn at a sharper radius. Completing the turn (E), Billy sinks again and pushes his knees sharply into the slope while keeping his upper body well out. That way he sets his uphill edges firmly, stops the turning motion, and begins a new traverse.

C

D

Billy Kidd demonstrates another parallel christie, this time with delayed shoulder, or counterrotation. He sinks slightly and prepares to plant his pole (A). With pole plant, and up unweighting, he rises, gets his weight forward slightly, and begins releasing edges (B). He leaves his uphill shoulder back to help him initiate the turn and move his weight to the outside ski. Billy's upper body is facing away from his direction of turning (C). While he has not initiated his turn with a strong counterrotation, as some ski techniques advise, this position does keep his weight on the outside ski of the turn and keeps him poised to control the radius. He finishes his turn with a sharp edge set of his uphill edges and is in good position for his new traverse (D).

to turn your skis. Try standing on top of a bump, and you'll find that you can turn your skis—parallel—in either direction simply by swiveling them or thrusting the tips from side to side with your feet. This is a technique worth practicing; it is extremely handy in bumpy areas, where you want to make quick turns without going through the extensive maneuvers necessary for the classic parallel turn.

TURNING FORCE

The force that turns the skis can be generated in many ways; rotation and counterrotation are simply the most popular versions of bodily efforts to deflect skis from their straight-ahead course. Skis can also be turned by "heel push" —shoving the tails of the skis outward at the unedged stage of the turn; by emphatic use of the ski pole; by "swiveling" or "tip thrusting"; and by many other means, including, of course, by simply banking the ski onto its edge and using the physical characteristics of the ski design to cause the ski to track in an arc.

The goal, in your early stages of parallel skiing, is smoothness and control. You can best accomplish this while you are learning by sticking to the simplest means possible. If you unweight your skis, release your edges, and then weight the outside ski of your turn, you will turn smoothly and with control. Once you've mastered that, you can begin experimenting with more elaborate—and quicker—methods of generating turning force.

EDGE RELEASE

In any turn across the fall line, what starts out as the uphill edge of the ski becomes the downhill, and vice versa. You must change your edging from one side of the ski to the other. In the classic parallel turn, this edge change is a gradual process, occurring over the entire sweep of the turn. Remember from your sideslipping exercises that you control your edges with your *knees,* not your feet and ankles. Envision your knees as the upper end of a lever, the fulcrum of which is your ski bottoms. By rocking your knees back and forth, you can rock the ski bottoms, bringing one edge and then the other into play.

Ski racers, called upon to make quick turns in series very close to the fall line, use their edges much more effectively than the average recreational skier. A racer will often set his edges with a quick push of his knees toward the hill. This edge set acts like an abrupt brake; the racer, carrying considerable momentum with him, reacts to this hard braking by bouncing—literally—from his edges, thereby using the edge set as a device to help him unweight. While unweighted, he cranks his knees in the direction of the next turn, which not only changes his edges for the next turn but also lays the skis onto their arc so they are ready to turn. The result is a succession of quick turns, a veritable dance down the slopes, that enables the racer to go through the closely spaced gates of a slalom course. The knee-cranking technique is a handy one—and a valuable concept for the recreational skier to keep firmly in mind.

Exercises for Parallel Christies

1. Practice the dry-land exercise, without skis, swiveling on your toes as described on page 74. Put in as many skiing movements as possible: the slow sink and rise of unweighting, the shift of weight from downhill to uphill foot, the change of edges necessary for a skiing turn. If you have the motion correct, your weight will travel, on a right turn, from the inside edge of your right foot and outside edge of your left foot, to the toes of both feet, to the inside edge of your left foot and the outside edge of your right foot.

2. Choose a gentle slope that you can schuss. As you go down the fall line, experiment with hopping the tails of your skis off the snow in a rhythmic series of hops in the fall line. Once you can do that comfortably, try hopping them

slightly to one side and then the other. This hop is an exaggerated form of unweighting—and by hopping to the side, you are doing an exaggerated parallel turn. Hopping is particularly good for getting you in the habit of moving your skis simultaneously and together.

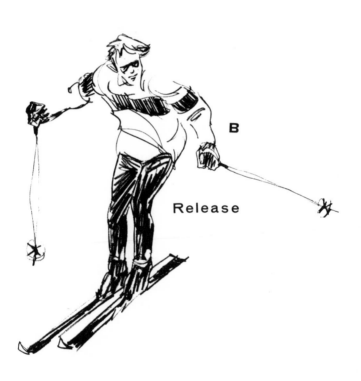

B

Release

Set

A

Set

C

3. Choose a gentle slope as in Exercise 2. As you go down the fall line, practice sinking down on your skis, bending at the waist, knees and ankles. Then spring lightly erect, straightening your body, and follow that with another sinking motion. Get the rhythmic down-up-down motion ingrained in your habits. Then, as you make your up motion, release your edges and displace the tails of your skis slightly to one side, then the other. You're doing a heel-pushing parallel turn, and you should be able to schuss the slope leaving a rhythmic snakelike track of gentle curves.

THE SKI POLE

So far, your ski poles have served principally to help you get about on the flat and to climb—you've probably been concerned with them in actual skiing only as they've shown a tendency to get in your way. Now you are going to start using them to help you ski better.

Your ski poles are used primarily as a *timing* device during the learning stages of skiing. You can turn without using them—in fact, as one more element in a confusing sequence to remember, the ski pole can be a positive hindrance to the learning skier. But once you've got the basic steps in your mind, once you can do all the exercises presented so far, the pole becomes a positive aid.

The pole is always planted on the side *toward* which you are going to turn. Think of it as a pivot point, around which you are going to make your turn. You'll actually make your turn several feet beyond the point where you make your pole plant, but the concept will help you understand the where and when of pole use. Reach out a couple of feet ahead and about a foot out to the side from your ski tips and stab and pole lightly into the snow. *When* you do this is a bit tricky, but once you've got the timing, the basic rhythm of skiing is yours forever.

Go back to Exercise 3 on this page. You are schussing a gentle slope, practicing the down-up-down motion of the

American Technique. You have learned that you sink slightly and then, as you rise, you begin your turn. Adding the use of the pole to this formula, the sequence is down-*pole*-up-down. You use the planting of the pole to trigger the initiation of your turn. You start your up motion and plant your pole almost simultaneously.

Pole plant for left turn: Billy Kidd has sunk down, preparing for rise that will unweight his skis. The pole plant comes at beginning of that rise, to trigger it.

Exercises for Pole Planting

1. Repeat Exercise 3, page 84, this time planting your poles alternately just before each up motion. Keep practicing until the rhythm is automatic.

2. Repeat the same exercise, this time planting both poles simultaneously. As you plant them, brace your arms and upper body and spring upward, so that your ski poles act as a pole-vaulter's pole and you actually rise off the snow each time you plant the poles, in an exaggerated hop. Use some muscle.

3. Repeat Exercise 2, but with only one pole at a time. As you alternate poles, really jam them in the snow and let the shock drive you upward. You'll find the pole an effective aid to unweighting. In fact, you should find in this exercise that you are doing a gentle turn each time you jam the pole, whether you are trying to or not! (Note: This muscular jamming of poles isn't recommended for your everyday skiing, but only as an exercise to accustom you to using your poles.)

To increase your confidence on very steep slopes, to give you more control in big bumps, try double-pole action. Here, Billy comes over the lip of a sharp bump and prepares to turn to his right. He jams in both poles simultaneously. The inside pole for the coming turn is planted normally; the other is set a little wider than usual, to allow for the turn to come. Note that the timing is the same as for a single-pole set—Billy has sunk down by bending his knees, and he is ready for the pole action to trigger his motion forward and upward to unweight his skis.

7
Putting It All Together

YOU now have all the fundamental skills of skiing. *Wedeln* —the tail-wagging succession of quick turns without edge set—is sometimes considered a final fundamental step, but it involves no principles not already covered. When you can do all the preceding exercises smoothly and competently, you proceed to the development of characteristics that can best be described as your personal skiing style. As far as fundamental steps are concerned, all you are interested in from this point on is perfecting the things you have already practiced, to do them more quickly, more efficiently and more smoothly, and learning to manage minor-key variations and adaptations upon them.

As you progress toward that efficiency and smoothness, it will help to keep a few key reminders current in your thinking. You will, for example, learn faster and ski better if you begin every skiing session—and undertake any new exercise—by *exaggerating* your body motions. Stay loose, and magnify and overdo your motions. Ski instructors do it, so that the movements in question will be obvious to their pupils; the same procedure applies when you are working by yourself. If you exaggerate, in effect you slow down the various body movements, since each movement takes place over a larger space and thus necessarily takes longer. If you can slow down the movements, you have more time to get them right. You will find, for example, that if you exaggerate the down-up-down motion for initiating turns, you will be unweighted longer and have more of a chance to get your skis turning.

Similarly, starting off each skiing session with a run in which you exaggerate movements serves the double purpose of reimprinting the necessary movements clearly on your mind and of helping you loosen up. Get loose, and exaggerate; you can get subtle later, when you have everything working for you.

You will also find you learn faster and easier if you will ski faster—and on steeper slopes—as you undertake more and more complex exercises. Some ski instructors tend to start each exercise on an almost horizontal traverse. That's nice; if you can do the exercise that way, you have really mastered it, and you'll be able to do it at any time, under any conditions. But for learning new movements, speed, momentum and a fair declivity are invaluable. You'll note that most of the exercises in this book put you in the fall line on a gentle slope. From the fall line, you don't have as far to turn your skis. Furthermore, schussing time—time spent running directly down the slope in the steepest way—is invaluable in developing balance and stability. Besides, it's more fun that way. Most good skiers spend a good proportion of their time almost directly in the fall line, making small short-radius turns from one side of the fall line to the other. The long traverse with a quick turn at the end is reserved for extremely difficult conditions. And for learning.

One other word of general advice. Skate. Skating on skis develops edge control and balance and is one of the quickest possible ways to get used to having those long clumsy things strapped to one's feet. Skate on the flats, skate up slight inclines and by all means learn to skate down the fall line on gentle slopes. The stability and control you gain from learning to do it will help all the rest of your skiing.

HOW TO HANDLE SOME SPECIFIC PROBLEMS

MOGULS. Moguls are those humps that grow in the slope because all the other skiers are turning in the same places. (They're sneaking their unweighting by using the bumps to initiate turns. They bounce over the bump and turn below it, which causes another bump. As a result, the bumps develop serially, and getting caught traversing across a long row of them will nearly shake your teeth out.) To handle moguls successfully, slow down and get your weight well out from the hill. Try to ski the troughs, between the bumps; when you must go over one, try to turn on its top and let your skis sideslip gently down the downhill side of it. Concentrate on keeping your downhill knee bent; if you lock it straight, you won't be able to absorb the bumps. If you get into moguls while moving fast, try down unweighting— quickly drawing knees and feet up under the body—to let your turns carry over the peaks of the bumps.

ICE. Eastern skiers cut their teeth on it; western skiers panic at the sound of "loud powder." Learn to spot the changes of color in the trails that denote ice patches, and avoid them if you can. Ski the sides of the trails, where excess loose snow is thrown up by the traffic down the middle. You'll do better on ice with a stiff ski, sharp edges and a stiff ski boot—edge control is *the* solution to stability on ice. If you see an unavoidable patch, get your weight forward —otherwise your skis will try to squirt out ahead of you —and your skis a little closer together, then prepare to push you knees hard into the hill, to keep your edges set. You'll be better off if you don't try to turn on ice. Run straight across it, and turn when you get back to softer snow. If

Coming into a field of moguls with considerable speed, Billy Kidd drops his weight down and gets his upper body out, for a sharp edge set to check speed and initiate a subtle turn to the left (A). Note wide-track stance for stability.

He skis the trough between two moguls (B) and goes directly across the top of the second, collapsing at the knees and waist to absorb the abrupt transition upward. He will plant pole on top and extend quickly on the downhill side to keep edges in contact with snow.

The turn in Figure C was begun on the downhill side of the bump in Figure B. Unweighted slightly on the drop-off, Billy cranked his knees to his left, turning the skis and setting the uphill (left-side) edges. In (C) his weight is well out from the hill (note angulation of body and delayed shoulder), his edges carving.

Billy stays in the trough (D), squares up his shoulders with his hips and prepares to initiate a turn to the right (ski pole ready to plant). He's reading the contours and taking maximum advantage of the terrain.

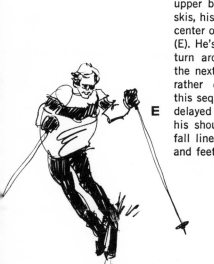

Finishing up the right turn, Billy's upper body again goes out over his skis, his knees pushed in toward the center of the right turn, to set edges (E). He's ready to carve a quick left turn around the downhill curve of the next mogul. What appears to be rather extreme counterrotation in this sequence is really a deceptively delayed shoulder—Billy is keeping his shoulders almost square to the fall line and letting his hips, knees and feet do all the work.

93

you must turn on ice, stem a bit; a stem turn takes less unweighting, and the severe up-and-down motion of true unweighting is apt to cause your edges to let go.

SOFT SNOW. Skiing real powder—the frothy, bottomless stuff that rarely falls in the East—takes a whole realignment of ski technique. In general, a good powder skier stays close to the fall line to keep his speed up, since the increased resistance of powder against the legs and body slows him down. He sits back slightly on his skis, in order to keep his tips planing back up to the surface. He *must* ski parallel; if he allows the skis to begin operating on separate

A modern ski expert cuts loose on the steep. Billy Kidd checks hard at the top, his weight well forward and out, his edges slammed into the snow distinctly (A). Simultaneously, he reaches forward for a pole plant, which helps him get his upper body out from the slope.

Rebounding from the hard edge set, he simply sucks up his legs and lower body (down unweighting), pushes skis out to the left, which banks them up onto their right-side edges, and carves a right turn (B).

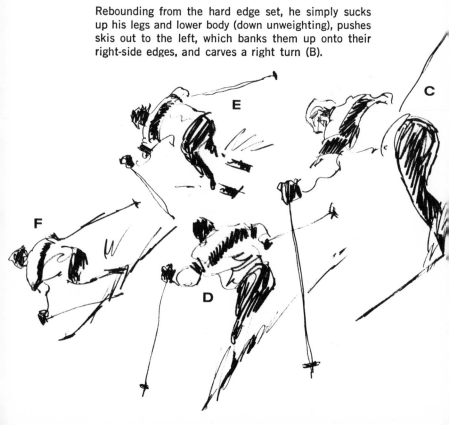

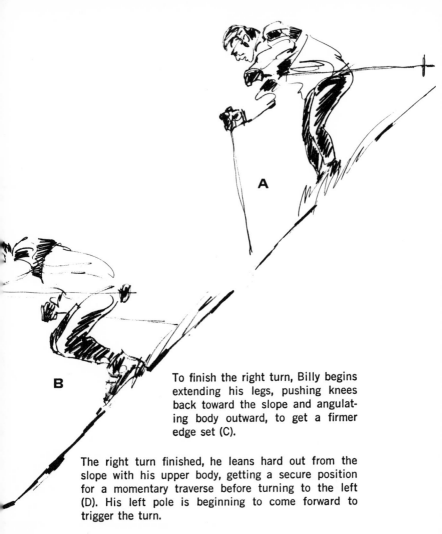

A

B

To finish the right turn, Billy begins extending his legs, pushing knees back toward the slope and angulating body outward, to get a firmer edge set (C).

The right turn finished, he leans hard out from the slope with his upper body, getting a secure position for a momentary traverse before turning to the left (D). His left pole is beginning to come forward to trigger the turn.

Using a small knoll for unweighting, he again collapses to absorb shock and to unweight, sucks up skis under him, then presses down on downhill side of knoll to set inside edges of left turn (E).

Billy carves out finish of turn, body re-extended, upper body out, knees ready to press toward center of turn to control radius (F). Zap, and he's gone.

planes in the snow, he is sure to fall. Exaggeration of movements helps, at least until one is accustomed to the sensation of skiing with the skis out of sight. Down unweighting is recommended. Even more to be recommended is lots of time and experience: deep-powder skiing is a special art.

For heavy snow, "wet cement," "mashed potatoes," the best generalization that can be made is that it is mandatory to unweight emphatically. You'll be more successful if you get your skis up to the surface on turns, in order to get them around. Hopping is no sin, in heavy snow.

FLAT LIGHT. On certain gray, cloudy days, or in falling snow, what fails you will not be your ski technique but your vision. All distinctions fade, and you suddenly realize how much you depend on shadows to help you read terrain. When caught by flat light (or fog), slow down. Ski the edges of the trails, near the trees or boundary markers, to give you some reading on how the slope goes. Yellow goggles also help.

STEEP SLOPE. Steep terrain is frightening at first; fear of falling is an inborn human trait. But the first time you really get your weight forward and out away from the hill, you'll find your fear disappears. Remember that you want to be perpendicular to your skis, not to the center of the earth. Once you get far enough forward so that is true, your edges begin to work, your weight shifts will be more effective, and you will find your skis quite easy to get around. Skiing very steep slopes is *easier* than skiing flat ones—if you approach them with confidence and drive. If at first you find extremely steep slopes disconcerting, try using both poles simultaneously; the double support will slow you down, reassure you that you have a stable base and keep your weight well forward, where it belongs.